to the finest fighting men i have ever known
grizzly co, forever
diver, forever
with love and gratitude

to k.d, t.c, m.s, m.r, and t.h
for encouraging, inspiring and refining me
much love, hombres

s o m e t i m e s
i g o a w a y

steven m callahan

DEAD RECKONING
20
17
COLLECTIVE

first edition | first printing

publisher: dead reckoning collective
book cover design: tyler james carroll
editor: matt smythe

printed in the united states of america

library of congress control number:
2025941324

isbn-13: 978-1-963803-08-2 (paperback)

"so understand
don't waste your time always
searching for those wasted years
face up, make your stand
realize you're living in the golden years"

wasted years - iron maiden

"i get by with a little help from my friends
i get high with a little help from my friends
gonna try with a little help from my friends"

with a little help from my friends - the beatles

fob: forward operating base 19

dfl: departing friendly lines 27

foreword

The day I graduated as a machine gunner from Infantry Training Battalion heavily shaped my perception of Marine Reservists. It was a warm, sunny day in late March. Along with one hundred and fifty or so other new infantrymen, I stood in our platoons at parade rest through a ceremony similar to graduating boot camp. The Camp Geiger gymnasium felt far less steeped in tradition than the Parris Island parade deck, and our MARPAT woodland utility uniforms were not nearly as crisp as the service alphas we would be changing into shortly to check in at our new infantry unit. The anticipation of what was to come next was fear and anxiety over how we would be treated by senior Marines waiting for us instead of excitement for liberty and the joy of reuniting with our girlfriends and families.

I am speaking for myself and those of us who were on active duty contracts. On this day, I realized that some of those who had been with me for the three months of boot camp and two months of infantry training had signed a far different contract. It was on this day that I first felt resentment toward reservists.

At the end of the ceremony, while they were hugging their wives, girlfriends, and moms, I was being marched off by an angry red-headed sergeant, along with the other dozen of my peers heading to First Battalion Sixth Marines. I remember getting back to our barracks area, where all of our gear had been staged to load onto the vans and buses taking us across the river to Camp Lejeune. All of the active duty privates were being talked down to and intimidated by the NCOs sent to pick them up, while all of the reservists might as well have just been handed their DD-214. At least, that's how it seemed to me, anyway.

My friends and I would spend that Thursday night cleaning a moldy, barren barracks room spotless again and again until the drunken Lance Corporals of Weapons Company finally decided they were ready to go to sleep instead of tossing our rooms again. I imagined all of the reservists I had gotten to know over the past five months, sharing our transition from recruit to Marine to infantryman. I remembered all the shared hardships from drill instructors, then combat instructors, the long hikes, the freezing nights, the mud, the heavy packs, and the uncomfortable racks. I thought of how my struggles seemed only to be just beginning, whereas they were probably back home by now, probably in bed with their girlfriends or wives, with their families, only required to do this one weekend a month for the next four years. *Fuck those pussies*, I thought to myself. Thus the distitinction between us and them had been drawn for me and all of my active duty peers.

I didn't see reservists again until the summer of 2018, about six months after my return from Syria with Charlie Company. We saw ourselves as proven, tough grunts who had deployed to an active combat zone in the late stage GWOT, where even the rest of our Battalion was on a non-combat deployment. A reserve infantry unit was to do a short workup on Camp Lejeune before going to Afghanistan. We sneered at and mocked the reservists as they would come and go from the barracks next to ours. At night, we would sit on our catwalks and get drunk, play loud music, and throw empty beer bottles at them in an attempt to instigate a brawl. Secretly, we were insecure about the lack of combat we'd experienced on our own combat deployment and envied that they were about to return to a life we had just been pulled back home from.

Infantry culture, and the military at large, is hierarchical and tribal by nature, and more important than rank in the hierarchy is suffering. The more you suffer, the tougher and more proven you are. It is unspoken, yet everyone understands. It is why we all felt ashamed for not having our Combat Action Ribbons, but proud for deploying. It is why grunts who don't deploy to combat but deploy once get social dominance over the non-deployed boots. And so it goes, on and on, down the pecking order.

A large part of my own writing dealt with the feelings of not doing enough in my short career, regrets, and trying to understand the effect that going to a combat zone and not fighting had had on me, along with the overall transformative process of becoming an infantry Marine in my late twenties. As I set out to use my voice to help change the narrative, I realized something extremely important – if I were going to heal from tying all of my self-worth to a pecking order that I had very little control over, I would have to extend that courtesy to all service members as well.

This mission to build community across the entire veteran population started Patrol Base Abbate, where I met Steve Callahan in the summer of 2022. Steve had been sharing his poetry, writing, and reflections on his time in Afghanistan through an anonymous Instagram account called Ashes of Helmand for almost as long as I had been running an account of my own and sharing the same. I had been a fan of his work for a long time, and we had spoken in direct messages on the app for over a year at that point.

Meeting an anonymous writer in person is often not what you'd expect. Steve was as thoughtful and introspective as I'd expect a poet to be, but he was also far happier and outgoing than I had pictured him. Although we initially connected over vulnerable writing about our darkest moments and thoughts, we fed off of each other comedically in person. He had a Sailor Jerry style tattoo of Marlon Brando as Don Corleone on his forearm, and when asked about it, he told me it was his call sign. When I asked why, he jutted his lower jaw out past his front teeth and made a perfect impression of the "day of my daughter's wedding" line from The Godfather that had us all in stitches.

By this point, Steve probably thought about his identity as a reservist far more than I did, which was not at all. The ego and pride we attach to our service compel us to compare and rank our service against others. I don't think of Steve as a reservist but as one of the best friends I've made in the veteran writing community. *Sometimes I Go Away* is the story of Steve's time in Afghanistan, his return home, and his struggle to move on to his next chapter. The poems in this book reminded me of where I had been and how I had felt just a few short years ago, and the journey that I had to walk to move on from those times when it felt like all that came left and right of bang would eternally revolve around a short period of time in a faraway place.

Poetry allows us to say a complex thing in a simple way, and Steve successfully does that in poem after poem as you journey with him through Afghanistan, home life, relationships, loss of loved ones, and personal struggles with identity after leaving an organization that prides itself on giving its members an identity that they keep forever. It is poetry that has allowed Steve, myself, and many others to become more than "just" a reservist, a grunt, a Marine, but something so much more profound – themselves.

-Mason Rodrigue

s o m e t i m e s

i g o a w a y

fob: forward operating base

forward. this word is multifaceted. in a literary sense, a foreword is an introduction to the work. but forward also acts as a fob, a place of rest and respite. if at any time while you're reading this the thought pops into your head, "goddammit, what is this guy talking about?" return here. this forward — this fob — serves as "my why." it serves as the foundation on which these poems are built. it serves as an azimuth, which directs the work ever forward.

mom

mom,
you should read this first
you'll come across
a lot of things
that you probably won't like

i say things like
f
and s
and talk about death
a lot

i understand
that you won't
and that's okay
its not your world
but peek behind the curtain

for just a bit longer
and maybe
just maybe
you'll understand
that i don't either

regardless of the uniform
i wear
you'll always see me
as your little boy
and when you come across

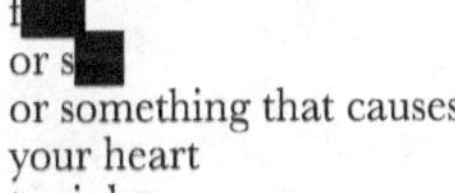
f
or s
or something that causes
your heart
to sink

and the hairs
to stand on end
come back to this
and remember

this saved my life
and most of all
the words i use
can't take away
the love i have for you

for the boys

we do it for the boys
for those who raised
their right hand and said
send me

who crawled through the barbed wire
of barbarism
who sat behind a desk,
who kicked in the doors

who took their weapon off safe
when the invisible monsters
in their minds
began their initial assault

who learned
over time
to put the safety
back on

we do it for the boys
who did it
for their boys
who walked their exodus

from marjah
and sangin
and ramadi
and fallujah
and vietnam
and korea
and saipan
and iwo jima
and belleau wood

for the boys who did not make this pilgrimage home on foot
but in flag-draped coffins
greeted with
runny mascara and
broken hearts

we do it
for the boys

we live
for the boys

we love
for the boys

we endure
for the boys

we did it
and will do it again
for the boys

my why

why do i fight
and i scream
and i rage
and i endure?

because you cannot.

my why
my answer to the pistol whispers
at midnight when i'm up to my neck in fear
choking on nightmares.

my why
why i fight the laughing
clowns of self-doubt the skeletal fingers
pointing from my closet

my why
the scream of fuck you
to the wall of silence
and loneliness

my why
because if i live on in spite of
the cold deep dark secret
places that no one will ever know

then you live on and
the light you brought
if only for a little while
will build a fire

that will burn on and
will warm my hands
as i plunge them into
the deep dark secret places of my heart and

the hearts of those
that suffer
like i do
like you did

you
all of you burning bright
snuffing out
became my why.

dfl: departing friendly lines

deployments are a mixed bag of emotions. i told my recruiter that i wanted to kill bad guys and so i became a rifleman for the Marine Corps. they only had a reservist spot available (as in they needed to meet quota and did what recruiters do) and so i had resolved — over a long period of time — that i would probably never locate, close with, and destroy the enemy. then i got the call. afghanistan. but, like fedora-wearing-white-knights, i did not, in fact, get any. this too took a long period of time to get over. i left my home, and the friendly lines therein, to stand in a box in the desert. i was hungry for the fight. these words a barometer of time in country. it was a hardline shift from normalcy of civilian life. my first day standing post, on that little combat outpost, that i grew to love (and hate), i watched several afghani children beat a cat to death with a shovel. several months before that i was standing in an air-conditioned gnc selling boner pills to old dudes.

you become something else

you become something else

a snake shedding its skin

    a sinner

    a winner

    a liar

a beast of a new nature

clawing at shriveled remains

of your chivalry and dignity

nothing else matters

    only fire and fury

    chaos and madness

    fear and loathing

from time to time when you walk through

the mausoleum of your memories

you'll stop at the unmarked

tombstone of who

you once were

and weep

almost, but no further

almost, but no further
i carry the torch
into worlds unknown
where darkness
and horror
and unspeakable dread
whisper honey-dripped doubts

almost, but no further
the promise land is not made for me
            wandering
                        wandering
                                    wandering
in the desert
for forty years
until my mind is
blank
and the old way
has died

almost, but no further
i will
            walk and
                        walk and
                                    walk
trying to
outlast the night
cold and dark
where the wolves howl and
will tear me apart if i am found

almost, but no further
as i have the enemy
in my sights
finger straight
and off the trigger
even though
i am ready to fire

almost, but no further
my time in the desert ended
and i returned home to
fight a different war

all this for a ribbon

all this for a ribbon
yellow
red and
blue
i stared into the desert
for hours
waiting for you
they told me
be careful what you wish for
but i only wanted one.
i was waiting,
but so were you
no combat
no action
no ribbon
not located
never closed with
i'm destroyed

backbone

9-lines and
addracs and
geometries of fires and
fundamentals of offensive operations and
mout and
reconnoiter and
call for fire and
air assault plans and
5 s's and a t and
the defense
three stripes up,
crossed rifles
in the center
(*backbone of the Marine Corps, sir*)
and an unbearable
weight of
responsibility
the backbone
must be strong, and
lethal and
the dumb grunt,
crayon eater,
asvab waiver
cliche
can kiss my ass

leadership

when i checked in
i idolized
admired
would've done anything
to prove myself
to my seniors

titans
madmen of war
nco's
who could do no wrong
you learn
that the gods

you raised sacred fires to
and lent field smokes
and drug your skull through the sand
for what felt like miles
just because
the command was spoken,

were human
and when i became
a squad leader
i told my squad leader
i get it now
and when i became a platoon sergeant,

i told our company guns
i get it now
and i do
i get
the rage and frustration
when the buddy rush goes wrong

i get
the joy of seeing your boys grow
i get the fear of seeing
a misstep
on a mock patrol as
a misstep

onto an ied
and how lit cigarettes
on fire watch
are target indicators
on post
and how your boys

you've watched grow
and laugh
could be taken away
in the blink of an eye
i get it now

starry nights in helmand

i think back often
as i'm prone to do
to starry nights
in helmand

my vision softens
no sleep for you
just starry nights
in helmand

the gunshots echo
the rockets roar
in starry nights
in helmand

i must let go
it's not my war
it's starry nights
in helmand

green eyed patrols
i loved the most
through starry nights
in helmand

there's no control
i'm back on post
under starry nights
in helmand

i think back often
as i'm prone to do
to starry nights
in helmand

my heart has softened
i miss it, true
those starry nights
in helmand

sometimes i go away, pt. i

sometimes i go away, my love
its not my fault, i swear
i signed the contract,
wrote my name
so i'll go
over there

sometimes i go away, my love
i have a job to do
and so i'll go,
and fight,
and kill,
i know i'll make it through

sometimes i go away, my love
off to a foreign land
i have this
reoccurring dream
of blood
spilt in the sand

sometimes i go away, my love
and one thing
will remain
that when i go away
my love
i won't come back the same

hadji-spn

i was deported once. it feels like a lifetime ago at this point. i had spent two years studying biblical theology in york, england. i fell in love with all of it. those gloomy days filled me with such joy, there was something so beautiful about the misery and rainy days where everyone carried umbrellas and wore welly's—or galoshes to those in the colonies—and no one seemed to mind. i had gotten an offer to serve as a missionary at a church in a town called king's lynn. the pastor and his family are like family to me (his son, one of my best friends, would've been my best man) and so it was a no brainer: serve god in england, with my best friend and his family. i had only been back in the states for a short period of time, but nonetheless, was able to raise funds through my local church, and set off on a plane to heathrow airport. when i arrived, i was subsequently detained and interrogated for several hours. it was me and several military-aged men with a certain middle eastern flair in a holding room. picture mclovin from *superbad* and a squad of taliban, and you'll get the idea. i ended up sharing jokes and drinking very bad coffee, and i slept for only a few minutes. for years after that when i was really tired, and drank instant coffee made with not enough water, i would flashback to that holding room in london, surrounded by strangers all waiting to be deported. now i'll flashback to helmand. i used to mix folgers instant coffee with grizzly straight and put a golf ball sized pinch in my cheek to get me through the long hours of standing in a wooden box, staring into the desert. post wasn't all bad. we had the sports channel where we stood, watching the ana play volleyball. across from post 4, in our little coop called bost (named such for the village of bost-kalay, which sat an uneasy 50 meters from the compound) was a large truck lot, owned by the afghans. at 1600 every day, they'd ritualistically set up a volleyball net and played until the sun set.

i called it hadji-spn.

春浜崎 (haru hamasaki)

the last time i saw your face
through an iphone screen
you were lucid and
said you loved me and
you'd see me soon
the last time you heard my voice

through a phone speaker
and mom told me later that
your face lit up and
your eyes fluttered
when i said i loved you and
that i'd see you soon and

when you died
a part of me died with you
not just because you were gone
but because i was off in a foreign land
thousands of miles
from home

without the luxury of grief
doing a job
that required extreme focus and
when mom called
i knew
before answering

i told jordan
(you'd have loved him)
my grandma's dead
and he let me take the call
mom told me the news and
i have hated being right

ever since and
i gave myself
the length of a cigarette
to mourn and
i still hate the taste of marlboros
because they remind me that

the part of me that died
wasn't just you
the part of me that died
was the ability
to mourn
you

oh three eleven

what is it you think i do? i asked
one day when she was unfortunate enough
to peek behind the
satin curtain and
caught a glimpse
        of the brute inside
        and when she stayed quiet
        i realized that i never asked myself
        what is it you think you do?
        we fight, yes
we kill, yes
we learned to tolerate
the worst imaginable conditions
and decompress with a cigarette
and bad jokes, yes
        we curse, yes
        we hike, yes
        the song and dance of
        the infantry on patrol
        is miserable step
after miserable step
through minefields in
marjah and
sangin and
helmand, yes
        we locate, yes
        we close with, yes
        we destroy everything in our wake
        for the sake of our brothers, yes
        but that is not all, no
for
we also love, yes
we laugh yes
we cry when our brothers and
friends are taken
        by the enemy or
        by themselves, yes
        we sing, yes,
        we dance, yes
        we hold sacred ceremonies
and share cigarettes
in the midnight hours
talking about everything, yes
yes, that's what i do

godfather

i made an offer they couldn't refuse

and could make my voice raspy

jut my jaw far enough

to look like the don

and we'd play the waltz

as my consigliere's

and i

would carry out

hits on the Marines

and our CO laughed

when i did it for him

and our 1st sgt looked at me

like i was a creature

covered in slime

but it was worth it

for the callsign

i received

would you rather?

we'd come up
with the most
fucked up ultimatums
in the field
drinking period blood or semen?
would you?
if you had to?

when i checked out
i played again
the stakes impossibly higher
would you rather
rise and trudge through the day
with an ILBE pack weighing 1000 pounds
or

take the long nap
rest forever
would you rather
fizzle out with a slow burn
cruising into your sixties
or

go out like a shotgun blast in a moment
would you rather
run into the unknown and
embrace every challenge
with wet cheeks and
wide smiles
or

leave behind a trail of grief and
sorrow for the boys to walk down
would you rather
hang your medals in a shadow box,
or

in a coffin buried nine feet,
cause deep down
you're a good person
would you rather
do the work and
make the change and

see the growth
or

spiral in misery's toilet bowl
for all eternity
would you rather
let go of the past and
face your future
or

build the straw dogs
of the best job
you've ever had
i'd rather
shine light into the dark places and
love them
than
wander into them and
hate myself

caffeine, nicotine, morphine

give me all or leave me be

caffeine, nicotine and morphine

to just survive i need all three

caffeine, nicotine and morphine

when i run hot through smoke to screen

caffeine, nicotine and morphine

to stop the thoughts that feel obscene

caffeine, nicotine and morphine

forgot about the place i've been

caffeine, nicotine and morphine

not here nor there, but in between

from caffeine, nicotine and morphine

rite in the rain

green notebooks

scrawls of

headspace and timing,

9-lines,

op orders

and edl

it made me laugh

to find

those things

that seemed so cool,

became commonplace

the first buddy rush and

radio you program and

range you run

are so holy

until you do them

a hundred times

and they become annoying

kerouac

on the desert road

wind causing my eyes to water

and how i miss those days

and how i wish i could go back

and how glad i am to know i'll never have to

oil tanks

my butt still puckers
when i see oil tanker trucks
on the highway
my knuckles grip

the steering wheel a little tighter
the sweat plays plinko
with the hairs
standing up on my neck

we were told "credible intel"
terry the taliban was launching an attack
they'd use an oil tanker
packed with hme

and we had heard this tired song
and we brushed it off
and we went out on patrol
and at three in the morning

the witching hour
where we heard the low rumble
off in the distance
jordan and i watched the road

where the high beams slathered the ground
in pale yellow light the tanker truck turned the corner
we threw a dip in the driver floored it
my heart fell out of my ass

so hard it cracked the concrete
we raised our weapons
clicked off safe
jordan drew the line in the sand

and the truck bore down
and my finger twitched above the trigger
and the driver slammed on his brakes
and flashed us a cheery as-salaam-alaikum

love conquers all

i realized

just the other day

that the foundation for war

    the brutal

    knife plunging

    bullet firing

    heart racing

    jaw dropping

violence that is conducted

like a symphony

is love

for as the book says

greater love hath no man than those

who would enter the gates of hell

itself

in place of those they love

somebody, to some people

i am not quite sure what it is,
but it feels like
an overwhelming pressure
in my chest like a whoosh
a rush of looking at the stars
and feeling
tiny
tiny
tiny
and i am standing
in front of the hall of fame
of the greatest men
i've ever known
and i am sitting in the library
reading for
hours
and hours
and hours
of all the stories
i'll never tell
and i know deep down
i don't belong like everything
i've ever wanted is a fingertip away
and i'm
grasping
grasping
grasping
but never reaching
i think its awe i'm in awe
that though i'm nobody
in this grand design i get to be
somebody to some people
and that's fucking rad

believer

a son of a pastor

who cherished the doctrines of faith

the means of grace

doing justice

loving mercy

walking humbly with his god

became

a son of a bitch

who cherished the doctrines of war

the means of destruction

doing violence

loving chaos

walking humbly as his god

inbound

bird inbound

head on a swivel

scan your sector

as moon dust

burnt trash

and the rancid smell

of death and shit

fills your lungs as you

breathe in

breathe out

to steady your nerves

sinners in the hands of an angry god

sinners in god's angry hands
midnight masses
general's plans
now i walk this lonely road
miles and miles
from my home
war is over damage done
stolen hearts
i'm on the run
moon dust kicks up from my feet
lawman wants
his way with me
suitcase full of endless lights
the dogs are loose,
they chase, they bite
my bones are cast like scattered dice
loves a gamble
for your life
behold the man hung from the tree
he looked for you
he looked for me
they pull the noose around my throat
death is waiting
and it gloats
can't go to the promised land
i'm a sinner in god's angry hands

one pump chump

i hope
i won't hang my cover
on the one thing
i've done in the marine corps
one pump to the 'stan
as a reservist is the
pinnacle of achievement
my life has to mean more
and so i busy my life
          to build
          and build
          and build
castles not made of sand
but of bricks
laid carefully
and with precision
          be
          here
          now
          build
          here
          now
the river flows
as it always will
and carry you
to the new and
the new
will be the now

shohna ba shohna

the war is over
and yet
ongoing

for some of us
we'd gladly carry the weight
for our brothers
then
why do we wait
for the worst days
to reach out
now?
we stood
shoulder to shoulder
then
why do we shy away
until dress blues and funerals
bring us back together
now?
we had
each other's six
then
wear
black bracelets
and get
igy6 tattoos
now
but it seems
to me
it takes too long
for us to truly
do it

forbidden fruit

bite the apple
live with sin
sweet
sweet
sin
the gentle trace of
demonic fingers down your spine
slithering
whispering
groans
of longing
needing
feeding
on your darkest desires
you crave violence
and blood
and you
will doom humanity
when your teeth
sink into
that apple's
flesh

oscar mike: on the move

when i returned home, it was a hard shift. i spent seven months in country; two weeks in camp lejune; and one week at picatinny arsenal. a week after that, after i had beaten red dead redemption and had very little left to keep me occupied, i returned to work at gnc. dumb grunt. when i returned to work at gnc, i had an out-of-body experience that i'll end this with. my first day back to work—again, 4 weeks after being in country—i tried to help a woman find vitamin c. she had asked for a specific brand that we were currently out of.

"i'm sorry, we're out of that one, i can either ship it to you, or we can find you a diff—"

"you're always out of everything" she thundered to me and a store full of things. she continued her tirade. "i come here for one thing, and it seems that everyone tries to sell me something different. you're terrible people"…yada yada yada.

i droned her out. *you stupid [redacted], you have no idea where i just was, and if i was shallow enough to tell you, you probably wouldn't care at this point.* she left shortly thereafter.

it is not easy to capture the reservist's heart. we raise our right hand in service; but we only serve part time. one day, when i am more mature, i will write "on the olympics of suffering" which is my philosophy on how some service members view service—the hierarchy is on-going and will continue, with my boots claiming that their boots "don't rate" for x, y and z reason.

afghanistan left its mark on all of us. i watched the tracers green glare and rockets bursting in air, which gave proof through the night, that i was not in ~~kansas~~ new jersey, anymore. i returned home to fight a different war. i was disgruntled and disillusioned by all of it. i wanted one, just one, notch on my belt, to prove to myself that my service mattered. it is an ongoing healing process. the dogs of war were not let loose, but instead were shackled in cages. i self-destructed. i self-imploded. i turned to drugs and alcohol to help me cope. i wanted to bite the bullet and check out early. i came closer than i'd like to admit. i went mad. i busted the drywall. i cried myself to sleep many nights.

the road to recovery has been long and arduous. it has also been beautiful. it takes time, but it is the fight of a lifetime. it is the fight that we crave, and i wake up every morning grateful that while these poems represent a "me" trapped in darkness, dawn will break for him very soon.

you will have bad days ***

you will have bad days

insane and alone

the only solace is the

thwup thwup thwup

of the ceiling fan above you

but you will have good days too

where the birds will begin

to sing their songs again

and the world will turn

broken crown

the king sits on
decaying throne
his crown
broken
the great, and strong and
mighty king, now
scorned
his scepter bangs the
marble floor
his hollow judgements
spoken
his subjects laugh
point and jeer
his kingdom
gone

the road i most travel

hurtling down some back road
100 mile an hour
high beams slice through
the ink-dark night

a golden circle
of suffering
and pain
in the middle of the road

forced by the fear of
driving to hell
alone
i bring you along for the ride

wrecking-ball

i wish my
love yous
could be enough
to tear down the
walls
i helped build
          brick
          by
          brick
i know
it will take time
i keep searching
for the right words
that will come through
like a
wrecking ball

peacetime

behind the berm, laying
prone in the hot
desert sand
waiting for the rock eaters
on the hill
to finish punching
holes in the enemy,
so our conditions could be set
and we could
        "move!"

and we let out a
war-cry to
wake the dead,
the spirits of
        chesty and
        basilone and
        daly and
        butler and
every Marine
living or dead
pushing us forward
as we crest the hill
to kill
        plastic targets.

weekend warrior

a tampon is what we were called
reduced to reservists
weekend warriors
semper sometimes

you go from a lion to a mouse
not the barracks, your house
put your shirt on not your blouse
just dating the game it's not your spouse

and all the while you hump your mile
you're on trial your lifestyle is not worthwhile
real Marines are hostile
you're in exile you're the x-files

you want to believe
you want to be seen
as lean and mean
not green service is in our genes

we aren't subject masters
but the biggest bastard,
when i get plastered
it's to face the facts and

realize the difference i made
wasn't paid to raid
i wasn't swayed from
the life of the blade

the life of the sword
ever forward
against the horde and
my few awards

pinned to my chest will always mean less
than those with whom i've been blessed
the guests themselves who've impressed
upon my soul in unrest in distress i undress

and stare naked at the world
my heart has unfurled
though my fingers still curled
into fists that twist at the wrists

ready to fight
but only in slight
only when the time is right
only when bathed in limelight

semper sometimes
with the weekend pull
semper part time,
never full

sorrys and goodbyes or: broken crown, pt. ii

have you ever
wanted to restart it all?
rewind the eternal clock
a few years
to relive or
undo
to go back
before
the tyrant king
returned from battle
to wage war
with himself
before
the kingdom
was pillaged
and razed
            and you
            you
you stood alone
and terrified
of the fallout?
i'd rewind it
just far enough
to watch you sleep
a little longer,
before i said my
sorrys
and
goodbyes

tis, tig

it all seemed

too much

and somehow

never enough

flashbacks

there was a river
that served
as runoff
for the compound,
and i hated securing
the lz
because
the birds with their blades
would
        thuppahthuppah
        thuppahthuppah
        thuppahthuppah
and blow
that bad smell
up the tower and
into my nose
then a goat
had the audacity to fall
into shit creek
        and die
        and rot
        and make
it so much worse
i still can't
shit in peace

believer still

a believer
born into faith
raised hands
wet eyes
looking to heaven
rejoicing
in the richness of our god
marveling at the mystery
and preaching the gospel of grace

the foundations crumbled
i stopped being
a believer
left with nothing
but myself to look up to
i lost my mind
i have prayed only once since
it was the day george died
i simply asked you why and
you refused to answer and
i have hated you ever since
i guess that means
i'm a believer still

sometimes i go away, pt. ii

sometimes i go away, my love
its not my fault, i swear
immediately whisked away
then i'm back over there

sometimes i go away, my love
its not your fault, trust me
a sound,
a smell,
a dream,
a fight and
i'm no longer free

sometimes i go away, my love
but only for a minute
still trying hard
to fight this war,
still trying hard
to win it

sometimes i go away, my love
i'm trying hard to stay
one day i'll beat
this fucking thing,
then i won't go away

20210816

i have been where you were
in your final moments
where the
unbearable weight
of living
presses so firmly on
the shoulders and
you cannot catch a breath
i have tasted the cold metal
of pistol
more times than i'd care
to admit
faced with only
loneliness and
horror
i wish i saw the signs
                    i miss you
we could've spread around
the weight
you carried
on the shoulders of
all of us,
together,
as we marched across
the minefield of your mind
but i understand suicide
for
it is easier to destroy
than to create
and sometimes when i
fail to cycle properly
and misfire
and send shrapnel into
the hearts of those
i love,
cracking open my
s k u l l
and painting
the walls with my
t h o u g h t s
seems easier than
doing the work
to untangle the knotted web
i wish i could've told you
how much better life can be
i wish i could've said
the right thing at
the right time
to show you that
it's beautiful here
and that
the storms will pass
i wish i could look you
in the eyes over a beer,
instead of looking at
your name on my wrist
etched
onto black metal
but above all
i wish you would have stayed

bukowski

i'm not convinced

that going mad

being driven to the brink

of insanity

howling in the midnight hours

rattling the bone cage

until the blood drips from your fingertips

isn't the only way

to find yourself

babe

she came second

that is the curse of being

able to

take pictures

with me in full dress

with my shiny medals

and a head full of hatred

for myself

for the enemy

wanting to die

wanting to kill

and no matter how much

help she offered and

hope she gave

i will take and

take and

take

command and control

your command makes it
or it breaks it
and they take it
and they take it
we have a call of duty,
but do we?
i'm honor bound
my honor's bound
tied up in twine
watching America
unwind
trying to right the wrongs
in my mind
tired of pretending everything is fine
i'm fine
the minefield of my mind feels less
like i'm sweeping
and more
like i'm keeping
the parts of myself
"you don't talk about at parties,
you want me on that wall,
you need me on that wall"
and crawling out of the hole
i'm whole
and my whole life,
a complete force redesign
i won't resign
no ua
i'm here to stay

golden years

golden years
come and go
in the field with the boys
huddled under a tarp
as the rain pelts down
like mortars all around
my miserable
mind only on the cigarette
"fuck this" someone says
we all agree
golden years
come and go
we couldn't wait
to leave the desert
missing home
missing you
i wanted to pet my dog
more than i wanted to eat
we couldn't wait to get out
so desperate
craving freedom
so badly
that we never realized that
the good times had
come
and
gone
and the best days
were yet to come

ribbon rack

my ribbon stack
finally grew
thanks, afghanistan
but cloth and metal, on my chest

do not make the man,
medals are not the only thing
i left that country carrying
now i have so many things

my mind has gone to marrying
now i howl at the moon in unholy midnight masses
now i can't help but see snakes in even the tallest grasses
now i jump at ghosts

now my ears ring eeeeeeeeeeeee
now i claw into the earth
and let out a ghoulish scream
decorations not on my chest

but on my heart
and mind
trying now to fix it all
and finally rewind

the spinning
spinning
wheel of time
that ticks along its path

the rage,
the hate
the violence
that boils

like god's wrath
none of it makes sense
and my mind
is finally shattered

broken
lost
and devastated
my ribbon rack in tatters

steven m callahan

while i was away

four of my pugs had died
while i was away
it left me feeling sad
but the job took up my day

my grandfather had died
while i was away
my hero now inside a box
and that is where he'll stay

my grandmother had died
while i was away
you got to be there with her
while i danced the war's ballet

a part of me had died
while i was away
i wish i could go back to find it
but my mind's begun to decay

i knew we needed time to fix it
before our special day
but you cared more about the vendors
and so i went away

tennessee whiskey

love is not measured
in giggles and sunshine
it is not measured
in just the good times
love is measured in piles of dirt
being shoveled away
to get to diamonds
it is measured
in the hard conversations
(the ones that piss you off and ruffle your feathers)
it is measured
in tender touch
after a gamble of vulnerability
it is measured in the long game
in its lifespan, not just the here and now
love is not always pretty
love is messy
bruised knuckles and cauliflower ears
from the knock down drag out fights
love is as smooth as tennesee whiskey
but she can burn like it too

drill foot

left foot
drill foot
right foot
kill foot
left foot
drill foot
right foot
kill foot
the endless march of the reservist
wanting to fight,
wanting to go,
wanting the night,
where the moon's softest glow
lets us go goonin
when the goonin is good
go kill for mommy
as a good Marine should
the kill foot is training
the drill foot our life
the dance of reservists
forever in strife

zeitgeist

everybody hates themselves
no one knows the truth
nobody demands the facts everyone wants proof
constantly infighting all backbiting
no one wins i don't think even Jesus
could forgive me of my sins

brothers fought and killed and died
in a godforsaken place
we were told to kill insurgents
to save the human race
now the fight is over
bombs hit closer, still at war

not one round was fired
but i'm more broken than before
politicians lie to me
a forked tongue of despair
i'm supposed to hate my neighbor
for his trump flag in the air

everyone's a sadist
there's no basis for the fall
we laugh at the world ending
but who's depending on us all?
bite sized tik-tok tic-tac mints
lets enjoy the show

a lion's roar of arrogance,
a mouse squeaks here below
art is dead and buried
we're not ready for the end
curtain calls me home now
and so i'll go and try to mend

here's good

what do you do,
when all seems lost
when the frost turns
green grass brown?

what do you do
when your life that you've built by hand
carefully planned, brick by brick
topples and scatters? does it matter?

do you take that long black road
where no joy is found
and the wayward trees consume the path? do you retreat?
going back to eat

at the table you've had
so many bad meals at?
do you idolize the past?
bastardize the future?

or do you walk
like that old wizard
one foot in front of the other
down the path of most resistance

trudging through the pain
through the rain of your tears knowing
that you're growing
and never wanting to stop.

kill

kill
kill
kill or be killed.
where saying goodbye is a luxury
that you can't afford.
        (kill)
where the thrill
becomes so total, you
        (kill)
inevitably load your hatred
and rage and discontent into your weapon to
        (kill)
fight the real enemy
where the world turns around but you stay still
        (kill)
where violence and gunpowder
are your star crossed lovers
        (kill)
where your lovers only exist in your mind.
where you missed the
        (kill)
war and turned that weapon
        ready to kill
        filled with hate
        filled with fear
        filled with dreams of the
        (kill)
glory you'd get pinned to your chest,
to yourself

battle damage assessment

maybe it ruined me maybe it broke my spine
and eroded my knees and
shattered my mind
maybe tornados chewed apart my house
            and ripped down my foundation
            and left me naked
            and confused
maybe i don't rate
these thoughts
maybe i should
embrace the suck
            it the fuck up
maybe it's nothing
maybe it's everything
maybe that's why i've locked myself away
from you
            (god how i miss you)
stuck in the storm cellar
waiting for the next gust of
wind to blow over
maybe then i'll emerge
            squinting against the sun.

rtb: return to base

we're almost there. can you feel it? we're almost out of the weeds. returning to base is about getting back to normalcy, getting back to a place of rest. it could easily have been called rfl, or reentering friendly lines. but rtb has a deeper meaning to me. it is a call to action. return. you've been carrying your pack for so long, maybe you feel alone? return. you have fallen off the wagon? return. your heart so fragile and delicate, smashed to pieces by a war or a woman? return. return to base, there's rest here, there's community here. oh, weary warrior, wandering far from home, return to base, and find solace once more.

fire walk with me

drawn and quartered
between two worlds
across the checked board
of time

i'm split
fragmented
yet somehow whole,
the steves are all in line
the pawns
and queen
a song
will sing
        you're free
        you're free
        you're free
the fires ceased
return to base
i'm un-castling
my king

frozen

let it go,
let it go,
the hate that has kept you warm
all these years
be calm,
courteous
and have a plan
to make the grass grow,
but know
the black flag is at half mast,
the dogs of war are nestled
in their cage,
the generals
no longer gathered
in their masses
the bell has stopped its toll
        now
        now
        now
it is time,
to keep your finger
straight and
off the trigger
and place
yourself
on safe

bygone

a bygone era
halcyon dreams of
chain smoking until
my lungs were raw
        such peace
        such peace
when the world was at my fingertips
and the words flowed
like the sweetest water
from a rock
those days are gone
there is only the now
the miserable
futile
beautiful
now
the past,
passed
bye,
gone

carry on

we played army in the woods
stick rifles and pinecone grenades our armaments
        fighting hordes of invisible monsters
        kids in hiding

we were Marines in the desert
rifles and grenades our armaments
        hungry to fight hordes of men
        monsters in smoke

we've come home from the theater of war
fear and rage our armaments
        carrying on against trauma's horde
        ieds in sand

steven m callahan

post traumatic growth

i saw a tree
the other day
while driving
down the highway

its branches
grew around
the wires strung from
pole to pole

resilient
strong and overcoming
i want that to be
my way

a seed can burst up
through the concrete
and life can
become whole

headspace and timing

i am an eleven
by trade
so machine gunnery
was new to me

in country i was behind
a 240
and a .50 cal
more than my m4

so i had to work on
headspace
and
timing

i'm a dickhead
by trade
so vulnerability and communication
were new to me

back home i was behind
arguments
and anger
more than love

so i have to work on
my
head space
and
timing

dd-214

finally free
after all these years
all these tears
all these fears

finally free
after all that time
all that chaos
all that's fine

finally free
'14 in hand
i went in a boy
i came out a man

i'm finally free
and that's enough
but saying goodbye
was pretty rough

return to base

the narrative
has been changed
we're here
no fear
get used to it
we aren't a time bomb
we are ready
ready
to relentlessly pursue
wellness and
excellence and
fill
sandbags
for each other
once more
we can
return
          to base
          to safety
          to freedom
of the self
of the horror
and violence
and face the world
with new eyes
and open palms
our future
bright and
though
sometimes we go away
we can always
          return to base

PREVIOUSLY PUBLISHED WORKS BY DEAD RECKONING COLLECTIVE:

FACT & MEMORY by: Tyler Carroll & Keith Dow

IN LOVE… &WAR: THE POET WARRIOR ANTHOLOGY VOL. 1

WAR… &AFTER: THE POET WARRIOR ANTHOLOGY VOL. 2

WAR{N}PIECES by: Leo Jenkins

LUCKY JOE by: Brian Kimber, Leo Jenkins, and David Rose

SOBER MAN'S THOUGHTS by: William Bolyard

KARMIC PURGATORY by: Keith Dow

WAR IS A RACKET by: Smedley Butler

THE FIRST MARAUDER by: Luke Ryan

WHERE THEY MEET by: Cokie

POPPIES by: Amy Sexauer

ROCK EATER by: Mason Rodrigue

REVISION OF A MAN by: Matt Smythe

ON ASSIMILATION by: Leo Jenkins

SANGIN, THEN AND NOW by Neville Johnson

A WORD LIKE GOD by Leo Jenkins

PHANTOMS by Ben Fortier

KILLERS IN THEIR YOUTH by Nicholas Efstathiou

DOUBLE KNOT by Mac Caltrider

DEMONS IN THE TAILLIGHTS by William Bolyard

ODYSSEUS AND THE OAR by Adam Magers

Dead Reckoning Collective is a veteran owned and operated publishing company. Our mission encourages literacy as a component of a positive lifestyle. Although DRC only publishes the written work of military veterans, the intention of closing the divide between civilians and veterans is held in the highest regard. By sharing these stories it is our hope that we can help to clarify how veterans should be viewed by the public and how veterans should view themselves.

Visit us at:
deadreckoningco.com

@deadreckoningcollective

@deadreckoningco

@DRCpublishing

@stevecallahan

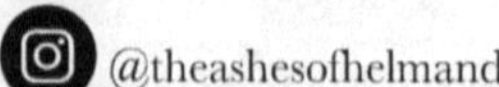
@theashesofhelmand

steve is the third most interesting man in the world. he once mud wrestled mud itself and was victorious. he dressed up like a marine for one weekend a month, two weeks in the summer and seven months in afghanistan. he skated under the radar long enough to earn the rank of sergeant and is very grateful to be separated from the marines (those extra two days really make a difference). he lives in virginia where he writes, works and cheers on the philadelphia eagles. sometimes he sneezes.

www.ingramcontent.com/pod-product-compliance
Lightning Source LLC
LaVergne TN
LVHW051004080826
845145LV00009B/2447